© Aladdin Books Ltd.

Designed and produced by
Aladdin Books Ltd.
70 Old Compton Street
London W1

First published in
the United States in 1984 by
Franklin Watts,
387 Park Avenue South,
New York, NY10016

ISBN 0-531-04770-9

Printed in Belgium

Contents

MAKE IT YOURSELF

Dinosaurs and Monsters

Consultant Caroline Pitcher

Illustrated by Louise Nevett

Franklin Watts
London · New York · Toronto · Sydney
1984

About this book

The projects in this book are designed for children to make by themselves or with a group of friends. Children can follow the sequence of instructions through pictures, whether or not they can read. The text is included for the parent/teacher to give additional hints and tips.

The "What you need" panel shows clearly what is required for each project. No supervision is required – except where this symbol appears △.

The materials needed for the projects are usually available in most homes or classrooms. Where certain materials may not be available, alternatives are given. It is a good idea to collect all sorts of household bits and pieces. See Page 30.

The level of difficulty of the projects varies slightly to cater to children of differing abilities.

Tracing

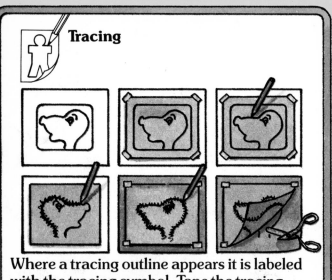

Where a tracing outline appears it is labeled with the tracing symbol. Tape the tracing paper over the outline. Trace the outline. Turn over the tracing and rub a pencil thickly on the back. Tape the tracing, outline upward, on paper or cardboard, and retrace the outline.

 Where this symbol appears, adult help is required. Look for it.

Cutting
Children should never be given sharp knives or scissors, and for most projects in this book they are unnecessary. There are many types of children's scissors available with rounded ends. Where objects are difficult to cut – for example, potatoes or plastic dish-washing liquid bottles – an adult should supervise. These instances are marked with the danger symbol. Where a plastic bottle is specified, be sure that it does not contain any dangerous liquids such as bleach or disinfectant. Always rinse out bottles, whatever they have contained.

Gluing
Any sort of paste or glue is suitable for making most of the projects, but in certain cases a strong glue is required and this is illustrated with a red asterisk on the glue pot. An adult should supervise when strong glue is being used.

Coloring
Most projects can be successfully colored with powder paint or ordinary watercolor. For shiny or plastic surfaces use poster paint, powder paint, or tempura paint mixed with a PVA medium. Look for the AP or CP seal of approval. Where projects are to be used in water, use wax crayons to color them.

Powder paint, poster paint, and wax crayons are all nontoxic and lead-free. Alternative coloring methods are colored pencils (crayons), or felt-tip pens and pastels. Ensure that the felt-tips you use are nontoxic.

One of the simplest ways of applying color is to cut out the required shape from colored paper and glue it onto the project.

What you need:

What the symbols mean

Glue

Strong glue

Scissors

Paint

Paintbrush

Wax crayon

Kitchen knife

Fat felt-tip pen

Pencil

Thin felt-tip pen

Paper

Thin cardboard

Thick cardboard

Tracing paper

Tinfoil

Pipe cleaner

Rubber band

Toothpicks

Drinking straw

Modeling clay

String

Coin

Cork

Cotton thread spool

Popsicle stick

Yogurt or cream container

Bottle cap

Small cardboard roll

Matchbox lid

Matchbox tray

Used matchsticks

Scotch tape

Small box

Large cardboard roll

Dish-washing liquid bottle

Knitting yarn

Milk or juice carton

Large box

- This project can be made from paper but it will be stronger if it is made from cardboard.

- Trace the outline in picture 1 carefully and cut out the shape.

- Remember that the dotted lines show where to fold and where to glue the serpent.

- Paint in a bright color or with lots of colors to make a pattern.

What you need:

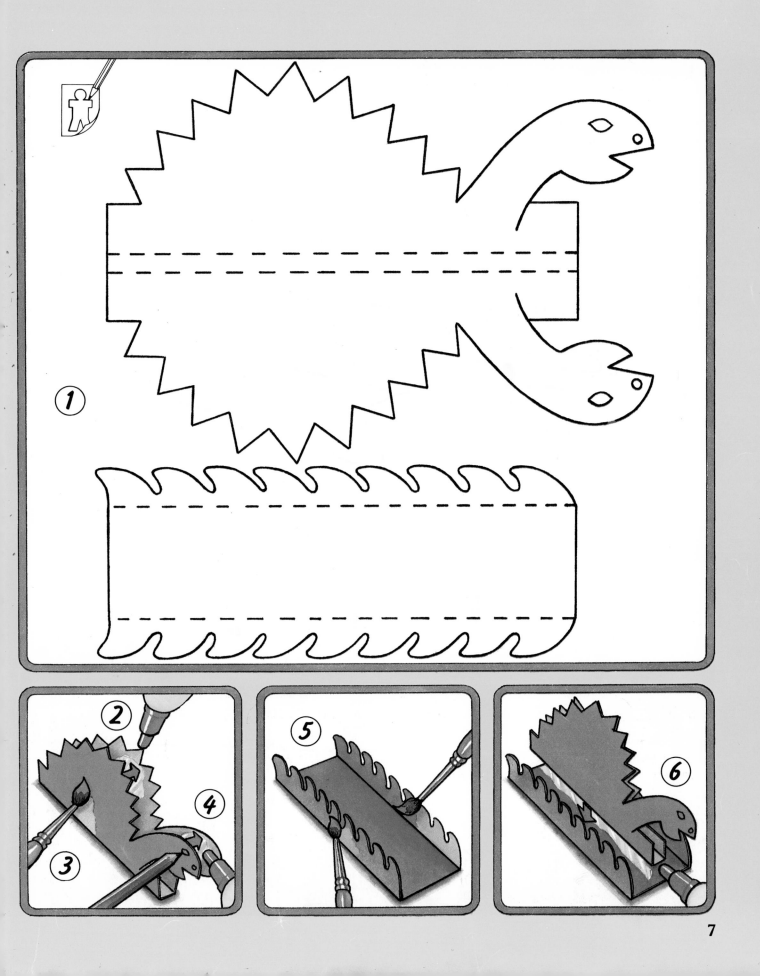

1

2

3

4

5

6

Dinosaur Skeleton

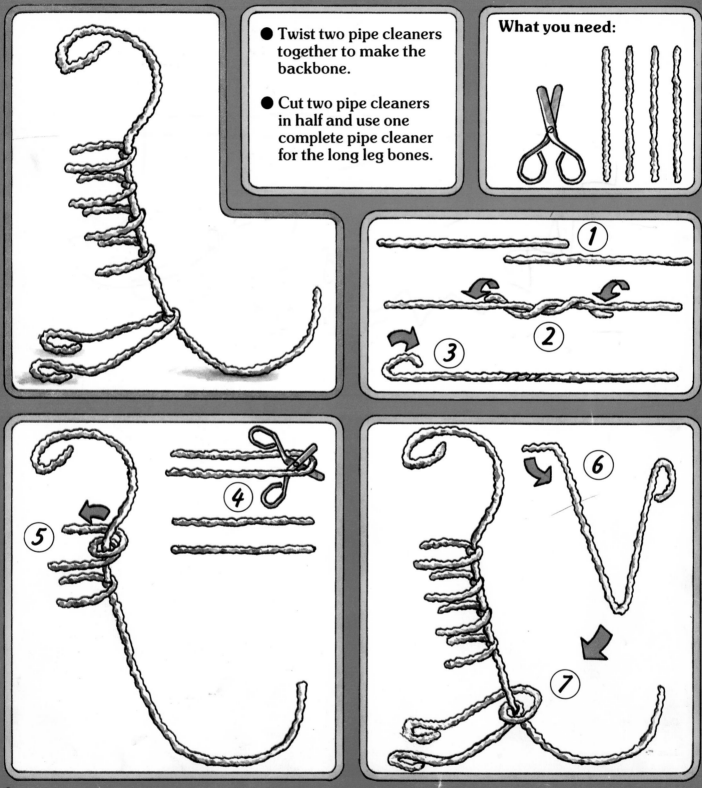

● Twist two pipe cleaners together to make the backbone.

● Cut two pipe cleaners in half and use one complete pipe cleaner for the long leg bones.

What you need:

Jaws

● Fold a piece of cardboard in two. Trace the outline in picture 1 with the bottom of the outline along the fold. Glue it to a piece of paper with waves painted on it.

What you need:

Cardboard Tube Lizard

- You need a long cardboard tube for this project – the sort of tube you find in the middle of a roll of paper towels – or you can make one by rolling a sheet of cardboard and taping it together.

- Draw and cut out the legs and spines as shown in pictures 3 and 6. Remember that the dotted lines show where to make folds.

- Cut out a tongue and roll it as shown in pictures 9 and 10.

What you need:

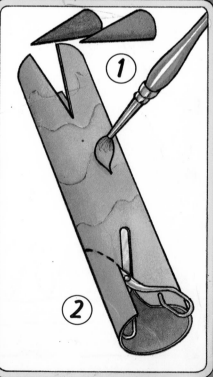

①

②

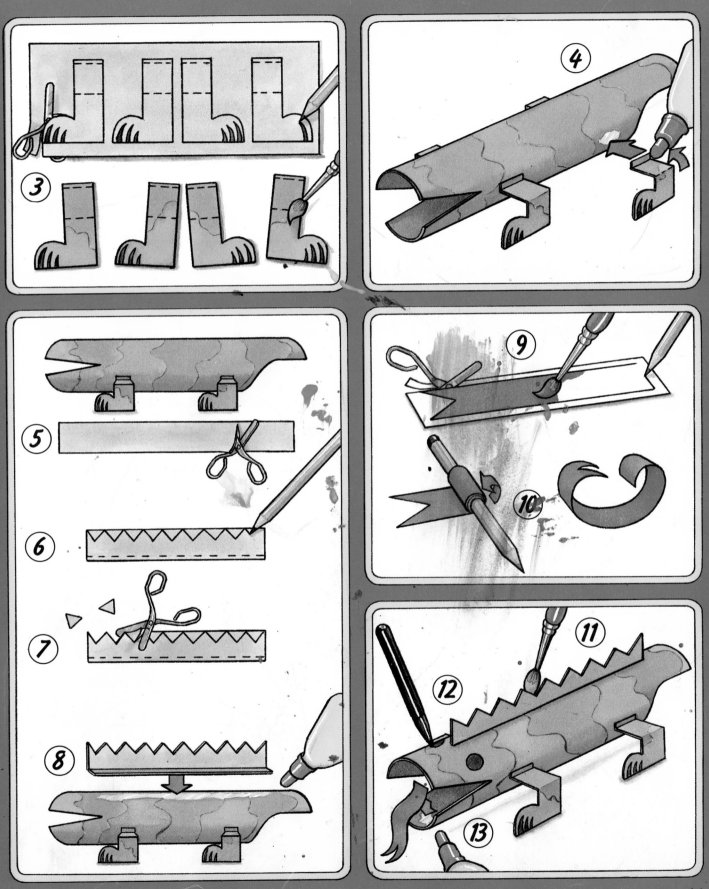

Cardboard Dinosaur

- Fold a sheet of cardboard and trace onto it the outline in picture 1.

- Make sure the spines touch the fold of the cardboard. Do not cut across the top of the two spines.

What you need:

① ② ③

Matchbox Beast

● Draw the neck and head of the beast on the inside tray of the matchbox and watch his neck grow as you push it open.

What you need:

13

Werewolf

- Draw around a plate to make the circle and add the ears before cutting it out.
- Copy the werewolf design and press out holes for the eyes.
- Cut around the heavy line of the nose and fold it back along the dotted line.
- Follow pictures 8, 9 and 10 for the fingernails.

What you need:

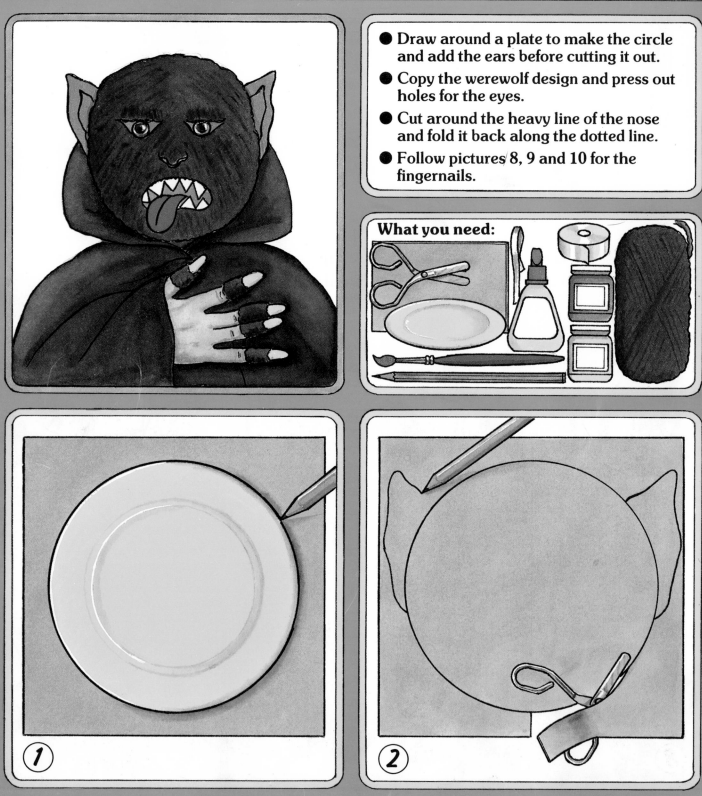

① ②

Carrot Dragon

- Children may need help in cutting the carrot. Do not give them a sharp knife.

- When making the long cut in the carrot, do not cut through too far.

- You can use circles of paper or tiny buttons instead of thumbtacks for the eyes.

- Toothpicks may be used for the legs instead of matchsticks.

- To make the spine, follow pictures 4 and 5.

What you need:

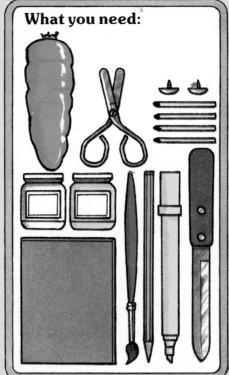

①

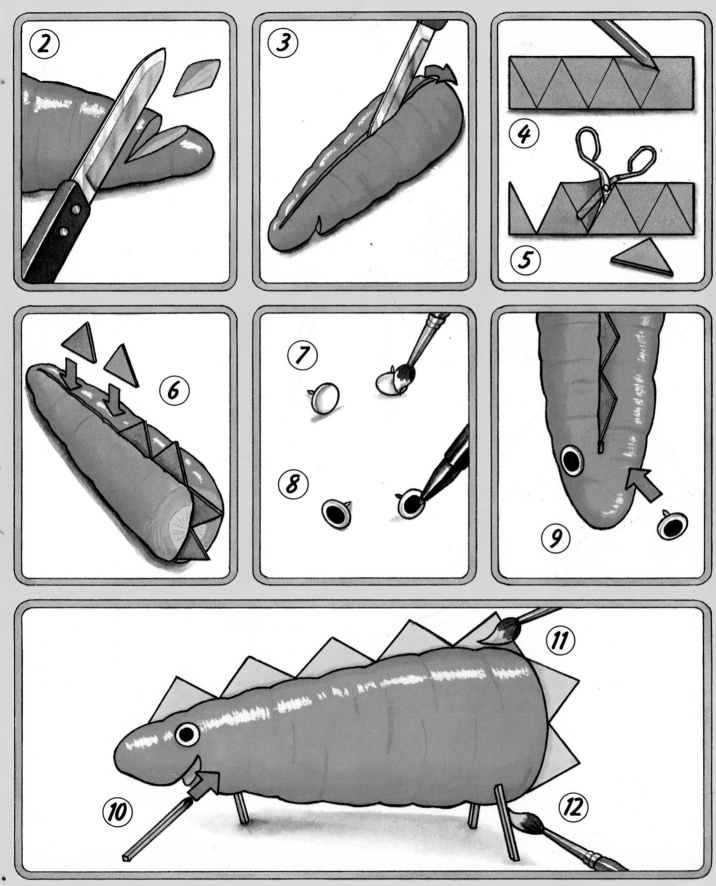

Balloon Monster

- Blow up the balloon.
- Add newspaper strips to flour and water paste.
- Burst balloon when papier mâché is dry.
- Use strong glue to attach the spines and legs on pages 20 and 21.
- Put newspaper into a paper bag and mold into shape to make the head on pages 20 and 21.

What you need:

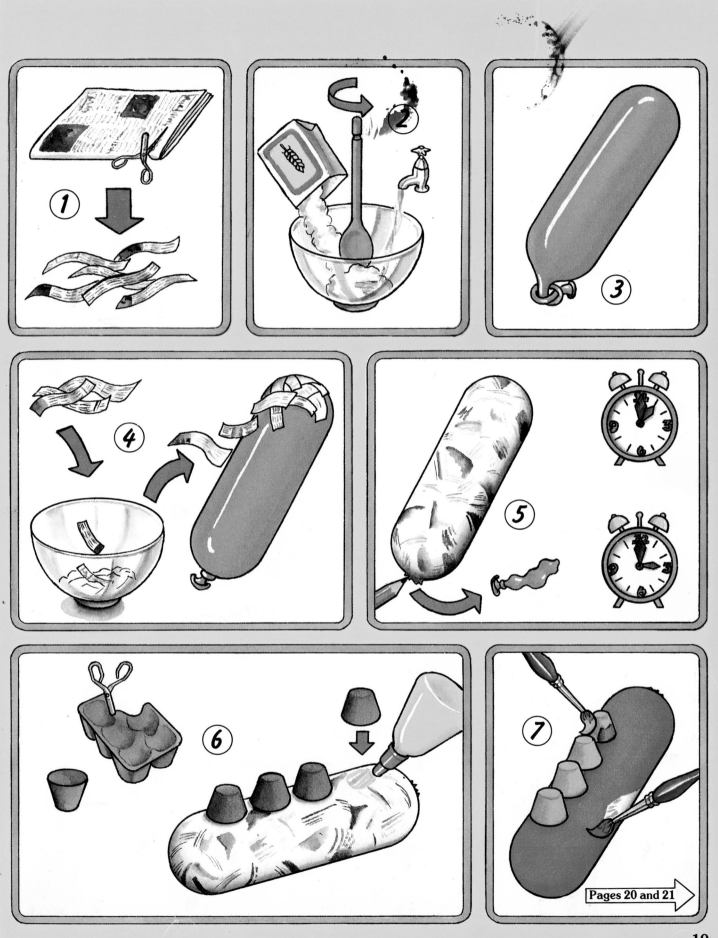

Pages 20 and 21

Space Monster

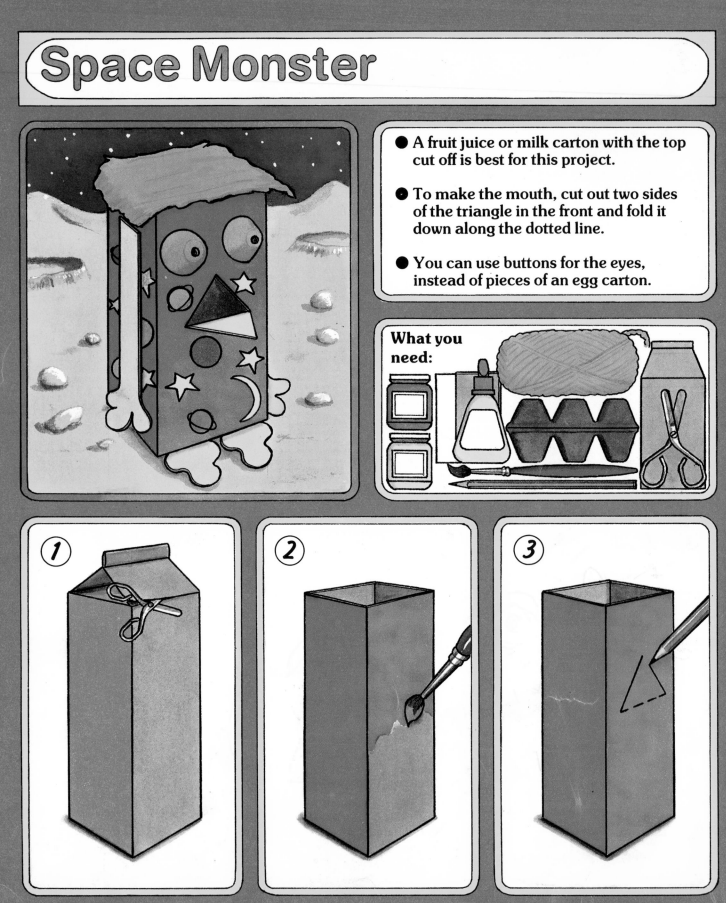

- A fruit juice or milk carton with the top cut off is best for this project.

- To make the mouth, cut out two sides of the triangle in the front and fold it down along the dotted line.

- You can use buttons for the eyes, instead of pieces of an egg carton.

What you need:

① ② ③

Eggbox Dragon

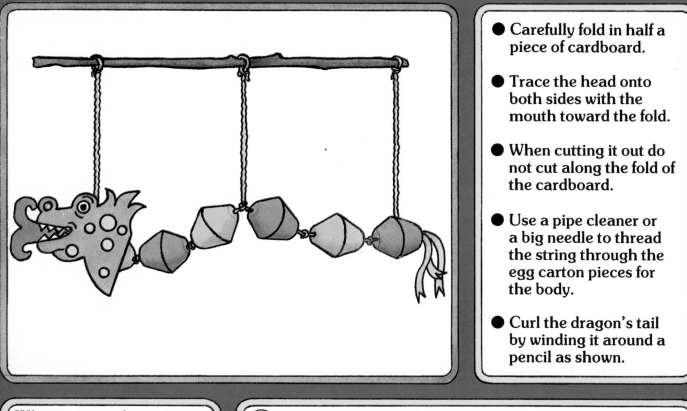

- Carefully fold in half a piece of cardboard.

- Trace the head onto both sides with the mouth toward the fold.

- When cutting it out do not cut along the fold of the cardboard.

- Use a pipe cleaner or a big needle to thread the string through the egg carton pieces for the body.

- Curl the dragon's tail by winding it around a pencil as shown.

What you need:

1

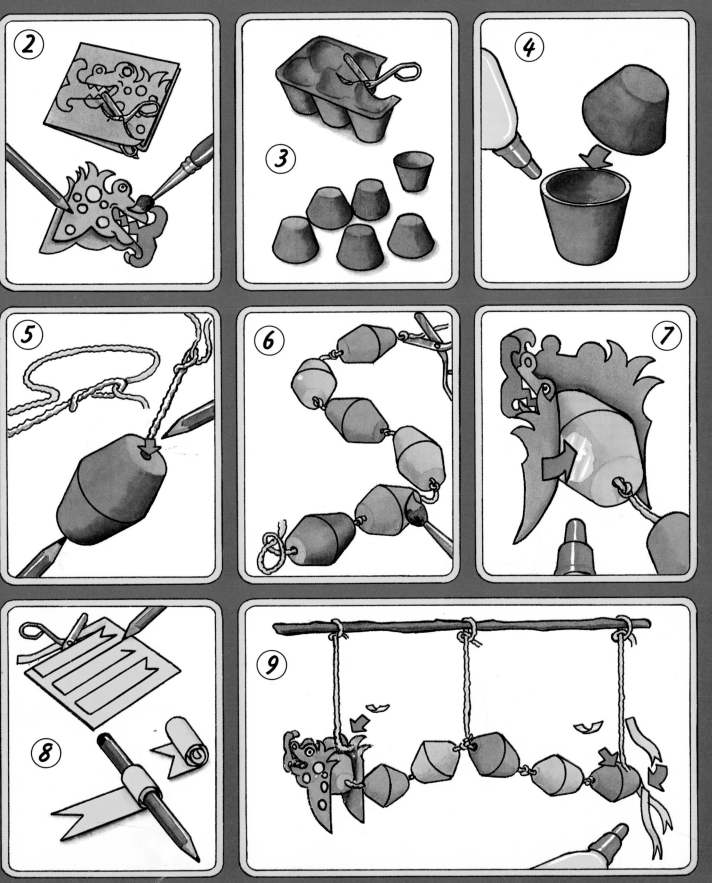

Woolly Mammoth

- Trace two circles onto cardboard using the outline in picture 1.

- For the head, wind as much wool as you can onto the cards.

- Small cardboard tubes are best for the legs, but you can make them by rolling sheets of cardboard and sticking them together.

- Trace two eyes, two tusks, one trunk and one tail from the outline in picture 15.

What you need:

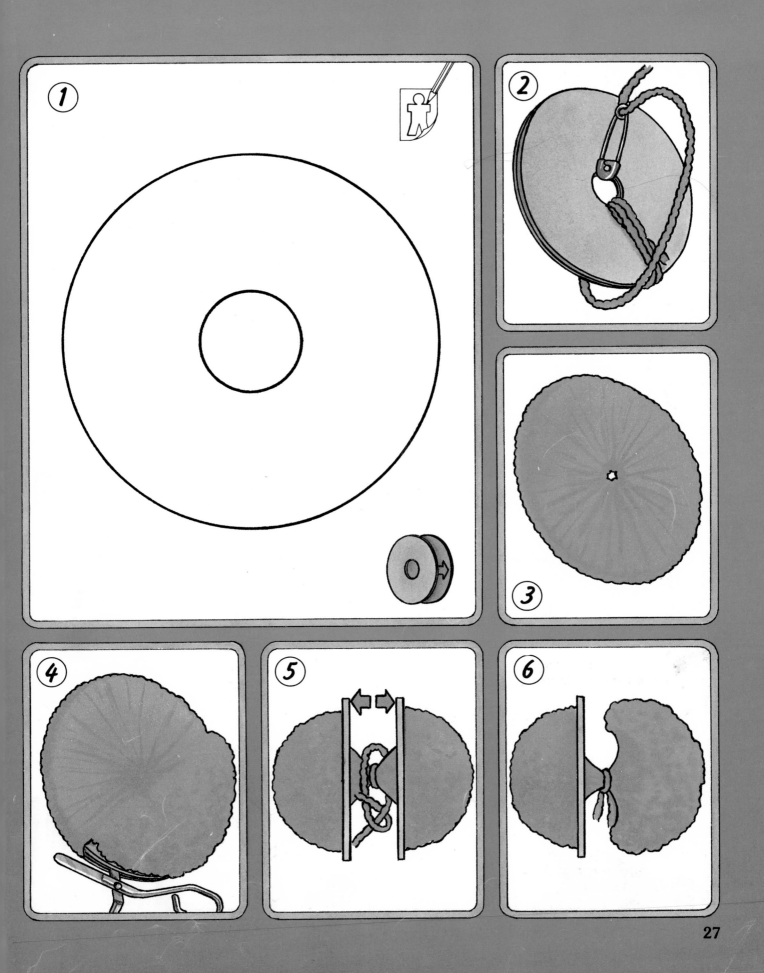

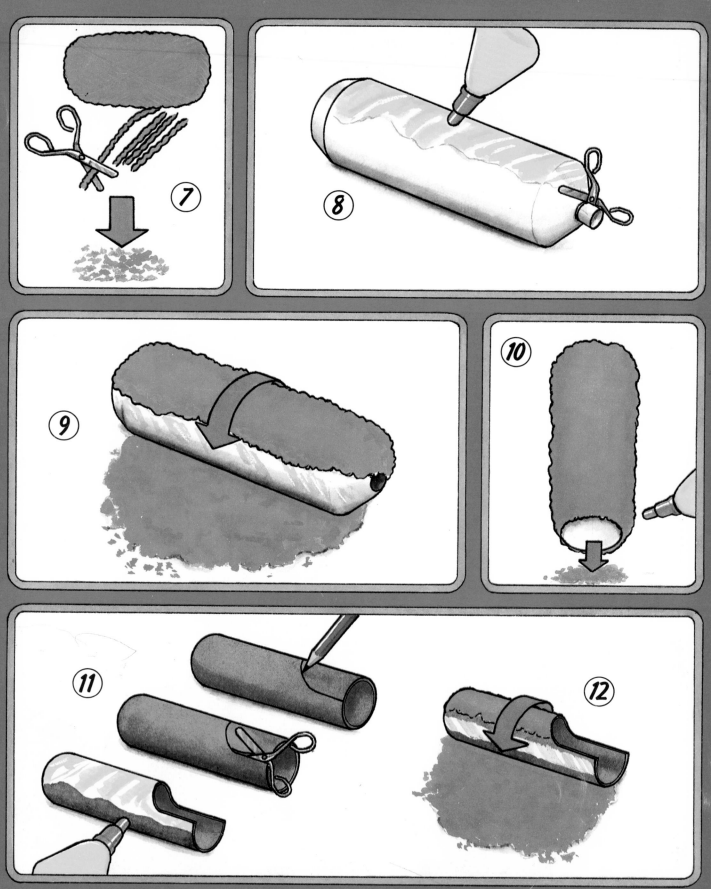

Bits Box

Collect all sorts of household bits and pieces on a regular basis. Children can use them not only for making the projects in this book, but also for inventing models of their own. Here are a few suggestions, but anything at all may prove useful with a bit of imagination. Keep everything together in a "bits box."

Projects conceived by **Aladdin**
Art Editor **Malcolm Smythe**

PRINTED IN BELGIUM BY

proost
INTERNATIONAL BOOK PRODUCTION